## Animals Animals Animals

# Polar Bears

By Alison Tibbitts and
Alan Roocroft

PUBLISHED BY
Capstone Press
Mankato, Minnesota USA

## CIP
### LIBRARY OF CONGRESS CATALOGING IN PUBLICATION DATA

Tibbitts, Alison.
　　Polar bears/ by Alison Tibbitts and Alan Roocroft.
　　　　p. cm. -- (Animals, animals, animals)
　　Summary: Discusses the physical characteristics, behavior, and life cycle of polar bears.

　　ISBN 1-56065-104-0
　　1. Polar bear--Juvenile literature. [1. Polar bear. 2. Bears.]
I. Roocroft, Alan.  II. Title.  III. Series: Tibbitts, Alison.
Animals, animals, animals.
QL737.C27T53　　1992
599.74'446--dc20　　　　　　　　　　　　　　　　92-11445
　　　　　　　　　　　　　　　　　　　　　　　　　　CIP
　　　　　　　　　　　　　　　　　　　　　　　　　　AC

### Consultant:
Jim Joiner, Senior Keeper
Zoological Society of San Diego

### Photo Credits:
Alison Tibbitts and Alan Roocroft: Cover, title page, 3, 7, 8, 11, 12, 19, 29, 30, 32, back cover

Mike Macri: 4, 15, 16, 23, 24, 27

Zoological Society of San Diego: 20

Copyright ©1992 by Capstone Press, Inc. All rights reserved. No part of this book may be reproduced in any form without written permission from the publisher, except for brief passages included in a review. Printed in the United States of America.

## Capstone Press
P.O. Box 669, Mankato, MN, U.S.A. 56002-0669

3

4

The land has no trees and the sky is often dark. Biting winds race across the green ice. Sea smoke blurs a distant view. This is a forbidding place for all but the most hardy. Solitary wanderers live and hunt on the ice pack. They are the polar bears. This is their home.

These bears are the symbol of the Arctic Circle. They wander over a vast territory. They have been seen near the North Pole. Some people call them "spirit bear of the north." Germans and Norwegians say "ice bear." Alaskan Eskimos know them as "those that go down to the sea."

The shade of their coats ranges from pure white to creamy gold. This depends on how sunlight reflects off of the fur's **outer guard hairs**. The color is good **camouflage**. Hunters and **prey** do not see the bear if he blends into his surroundings.

The animals keep warm in several ways. Air gets trapped inside the outer guard hairs. The sun heats this air into a snug blanket. A soft and oily undercoat holds body heat. Many **vessels** in the back carry warm blood through the body. A thick layer of fat also protects from the cold.

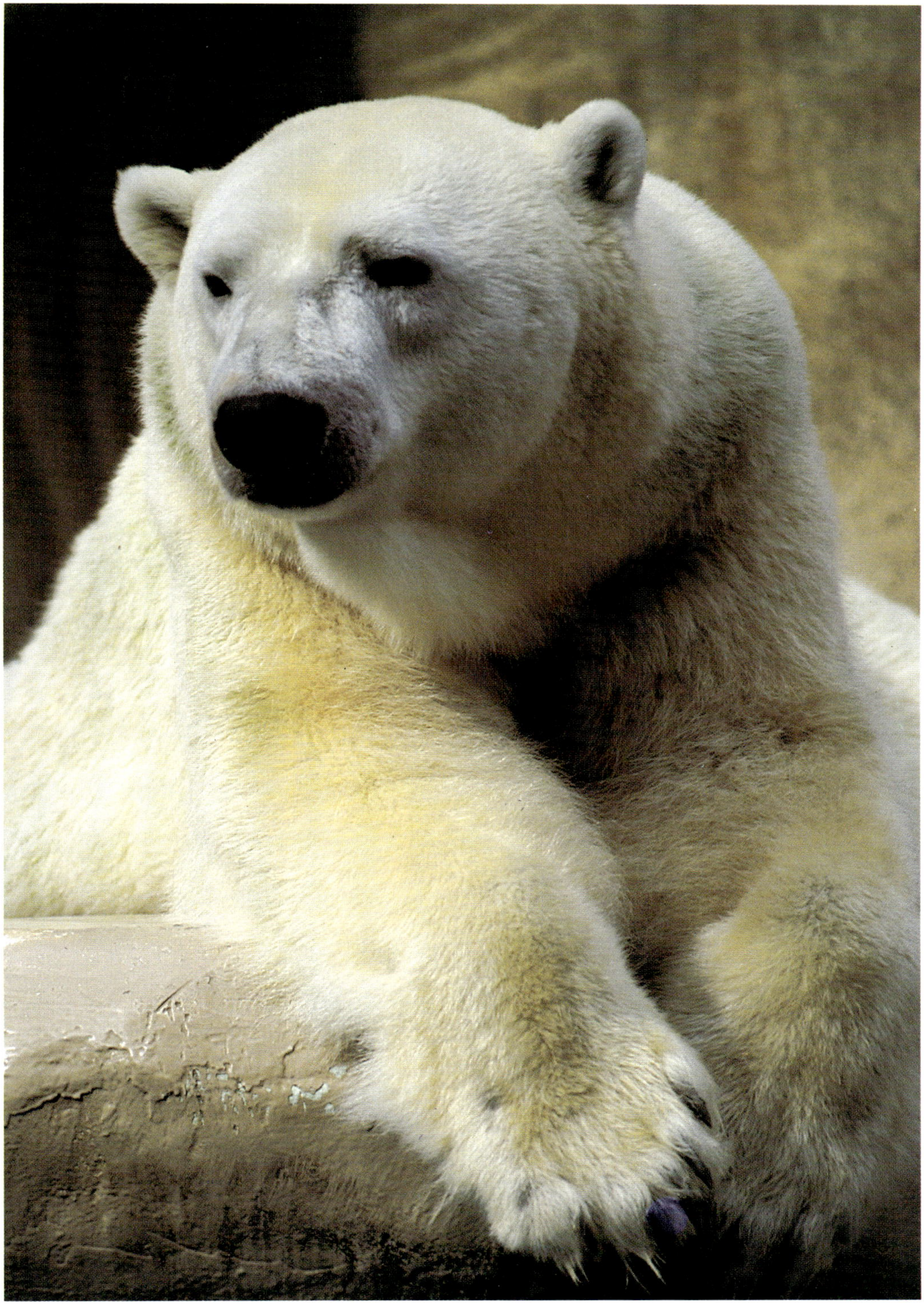

8

Males tower two feet over females and weigh twice as much. They both have slender necks. The narrow heads have sloped faces. Their eyes see poorly, but polar bear noses can smell prey twenty miles away. The bears stand on their hind legs and sniff to check the direction of the prey's scent.

Polar bears have huge feet. The back ones are twice as big as those in front. These are the only bears with webbed front toes to help them swim. Thick hair covers the bottoms of their feet. Rough "non-skid" pads in the hair give strong **traction**. Long, sharp claws grip ice and prey firmly.

These animals are the world's largest meat eaters. They are clever hunters and feed every few days. In the water, they appear to be chunks of floating ice. They glide slowly toward their prey as it sits on the ice. On land, they crouch down and crawl on their stomachs. They sometimes put a paw over their black nose to hide the color.

Ringed seals are their favorite prey. These animals live around **ice floes** and breathe air through holes in the ice. A hungry bear will close all but one of the seal's holes. The bear stays next to the last open hole and waits for the seal. It will sit patiently for hours. The bear is so strong it can jerk an adult seal through a hole as small as a dinner plate. It eats the skin and blubber. Arctic foxes and seagulls gobble the leftovers.

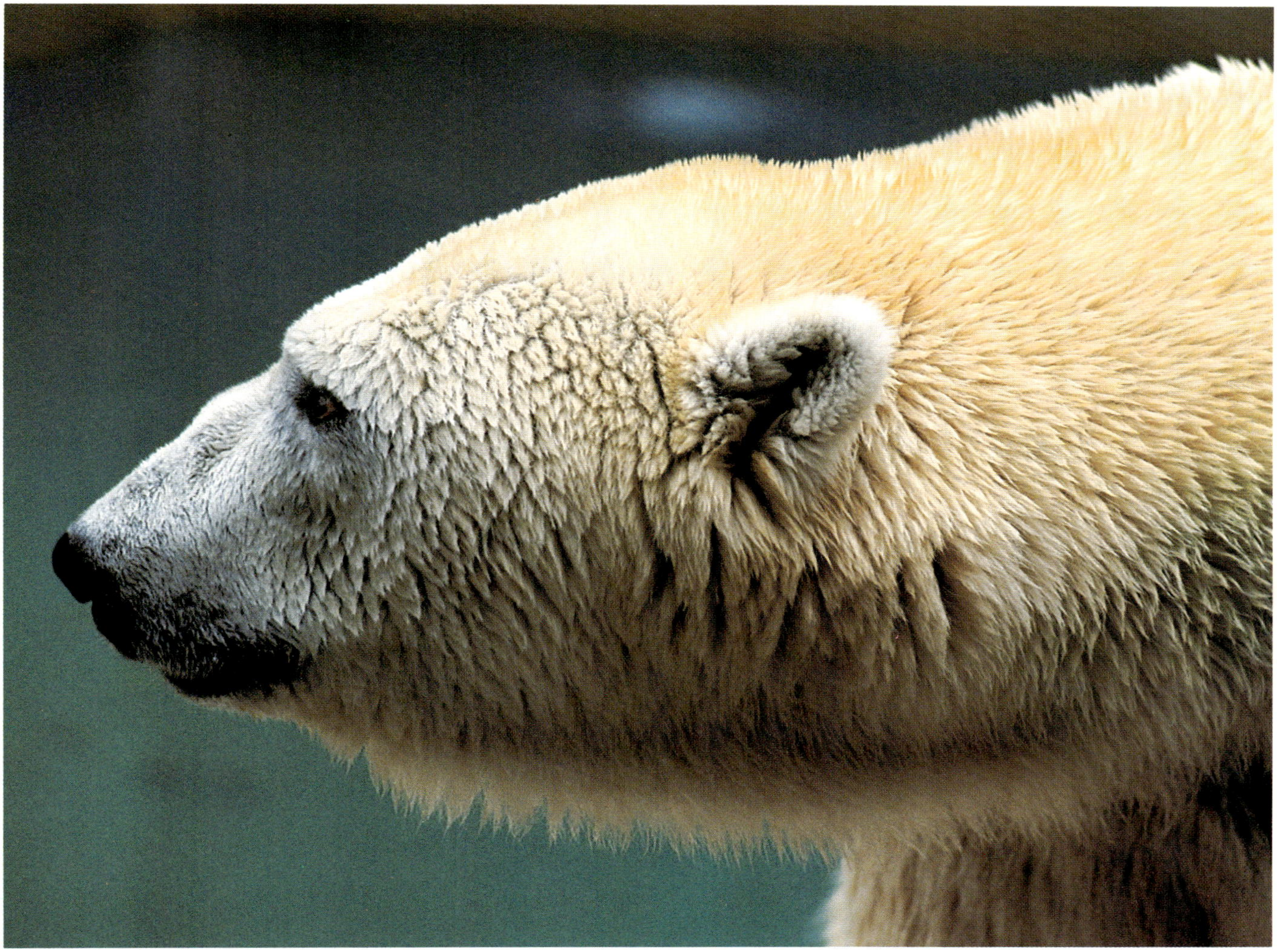

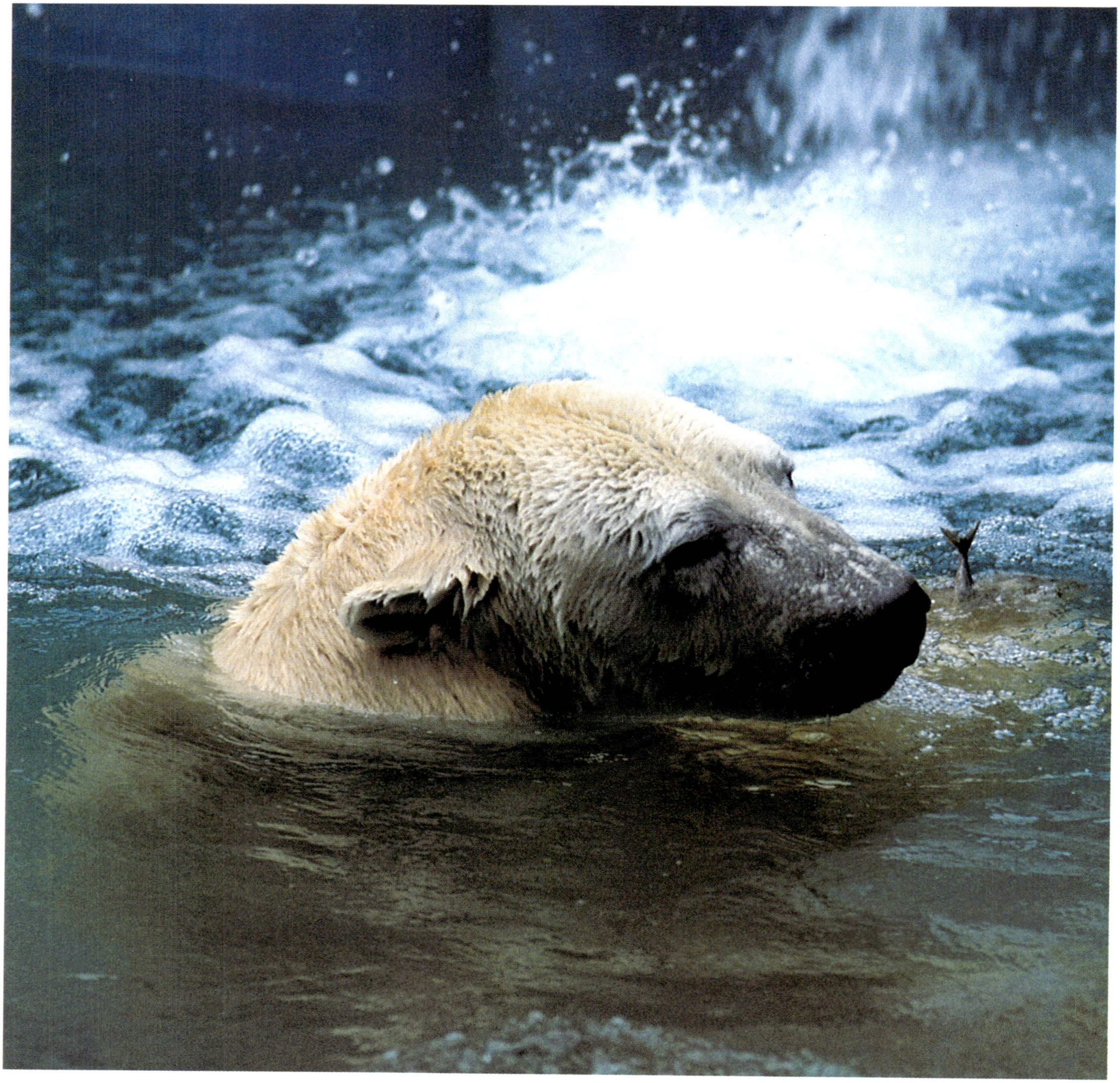

A polar bear spends half of its life in the water. An ocean swim might stretch over a hundred miles. A dive can last for two minutes and go fifteen feet down. It is hard for this **pigeon-toed** animal to move on land. It out-runs a man for a short distance. Then it must stop to cool down.

Breeding and **migration** are social seasons. Canadian polar bears spend the winter on Hudson Bay. In mid-summer they ride melting ice floes south to land. For weeks they eat kelp, carrion, sea birds, and berries in the woods.

Migration north to the ice pack begins in October. Over one thousand animals travel in the world's largest polar bear group. They follow the shore of Hudson Bay and pass the town of Churchill. The bears have come along this trail for thousands of years.

Animals and people watch each other for eight weeks. Hungry bears eat what and where they can. They get muddy visiting the town's garbage dump. Some bears return every year and bring their babies. This is where they all learn about fire.

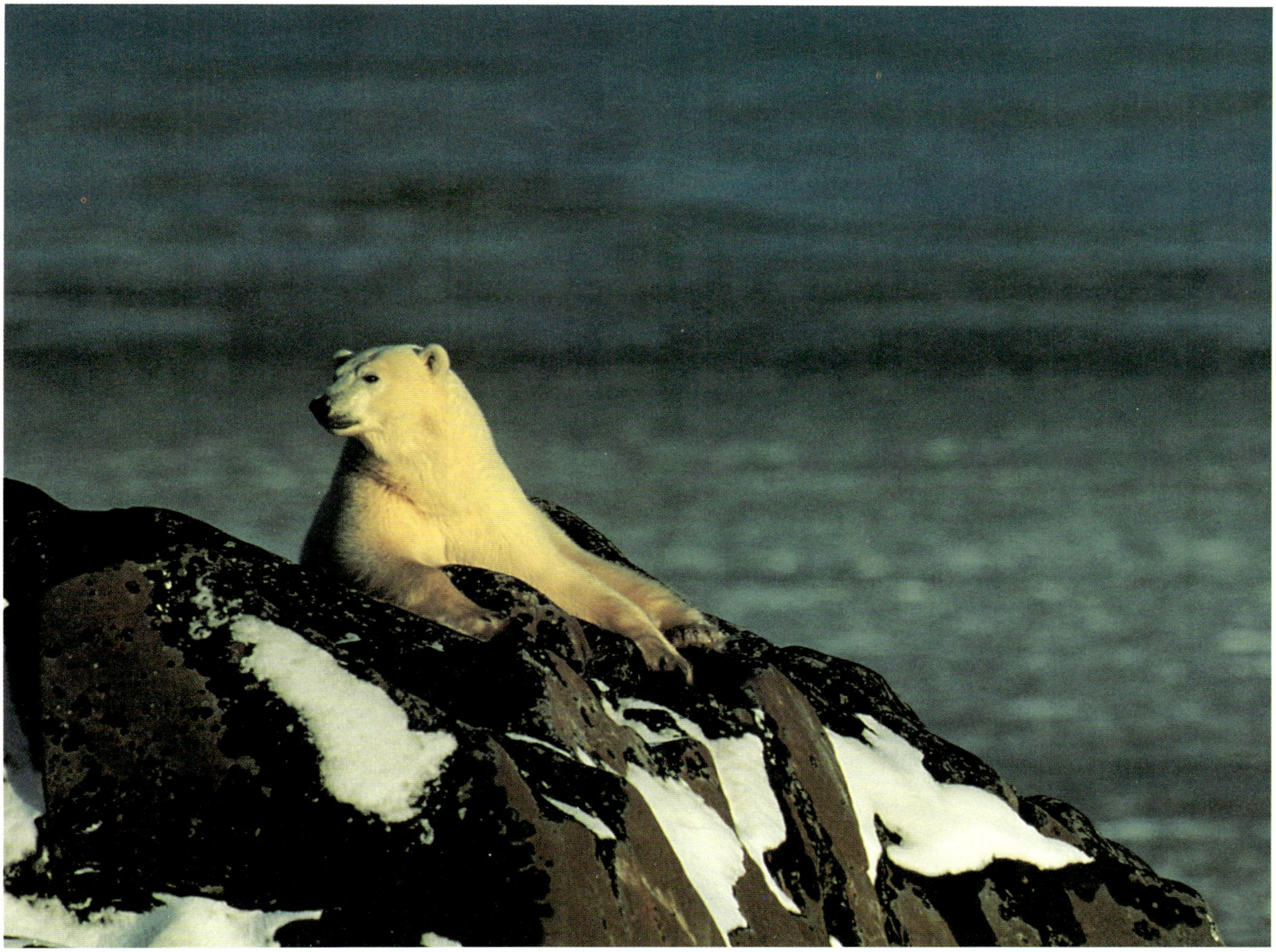

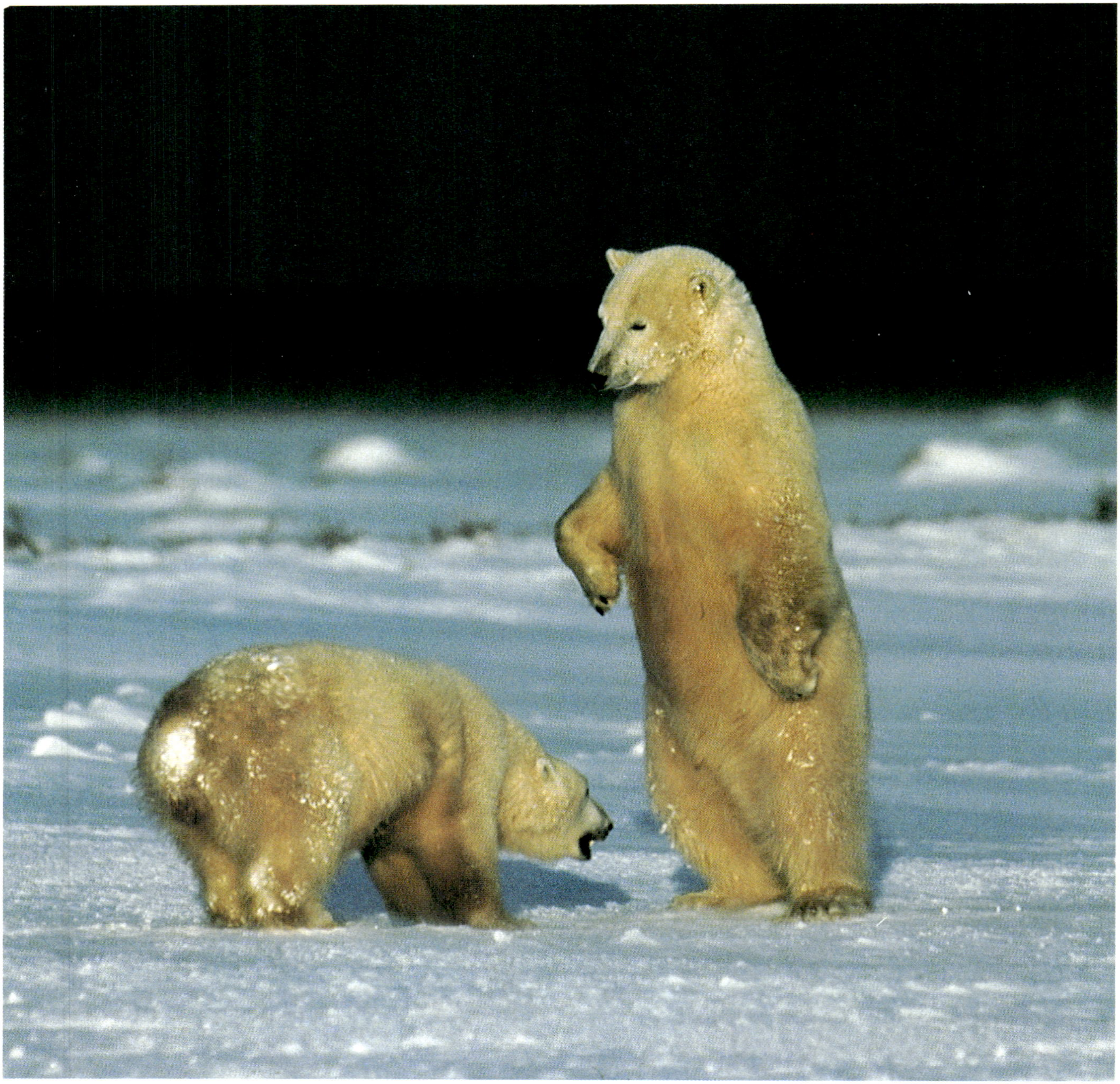

The residents of Churchill believe "a safe polar bear is a distant polar bear." They know the animals are unpredictable and dangerous. Hisses and snorts warn of an attack. Children learn how to "play dead" in case they meet a bear. Problem animals are trapped. Helicopters fly them far from the town and release them onto the ice.

Females expecting cubs den up to wait for their babies. They dig caves in deep snowdrifts. The space inside is not much bigger than they are. The entrance tunnel is below the roof of the cave. Trapped air keeps the den warm. The sows, or female bears, do not eat for three or four months. They breathe more slowly as their body temperature lowers. They are not in true **hibernation**. Polar bears do not hibernate. Some sows have come hundreds of miles to den up where they were born.

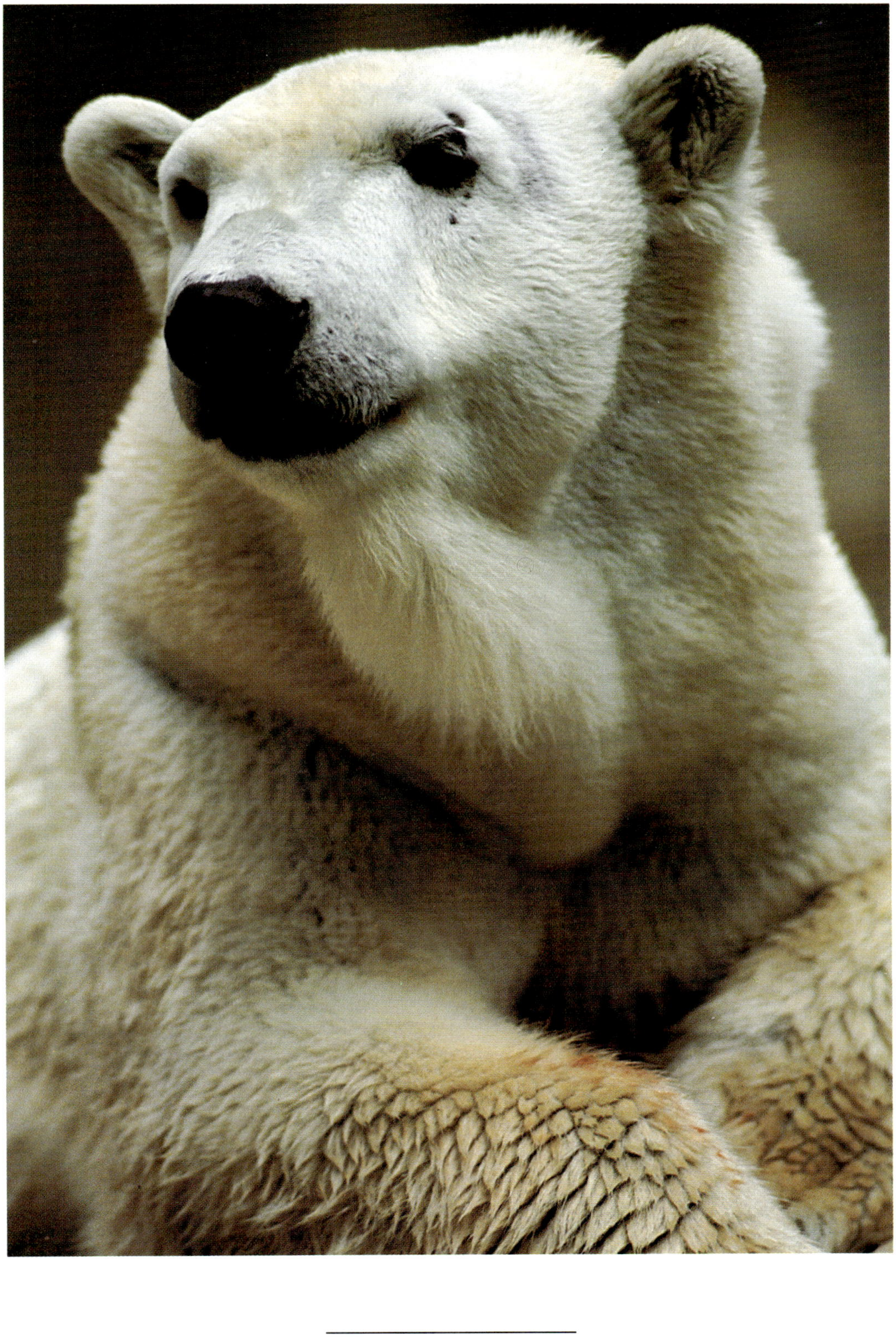

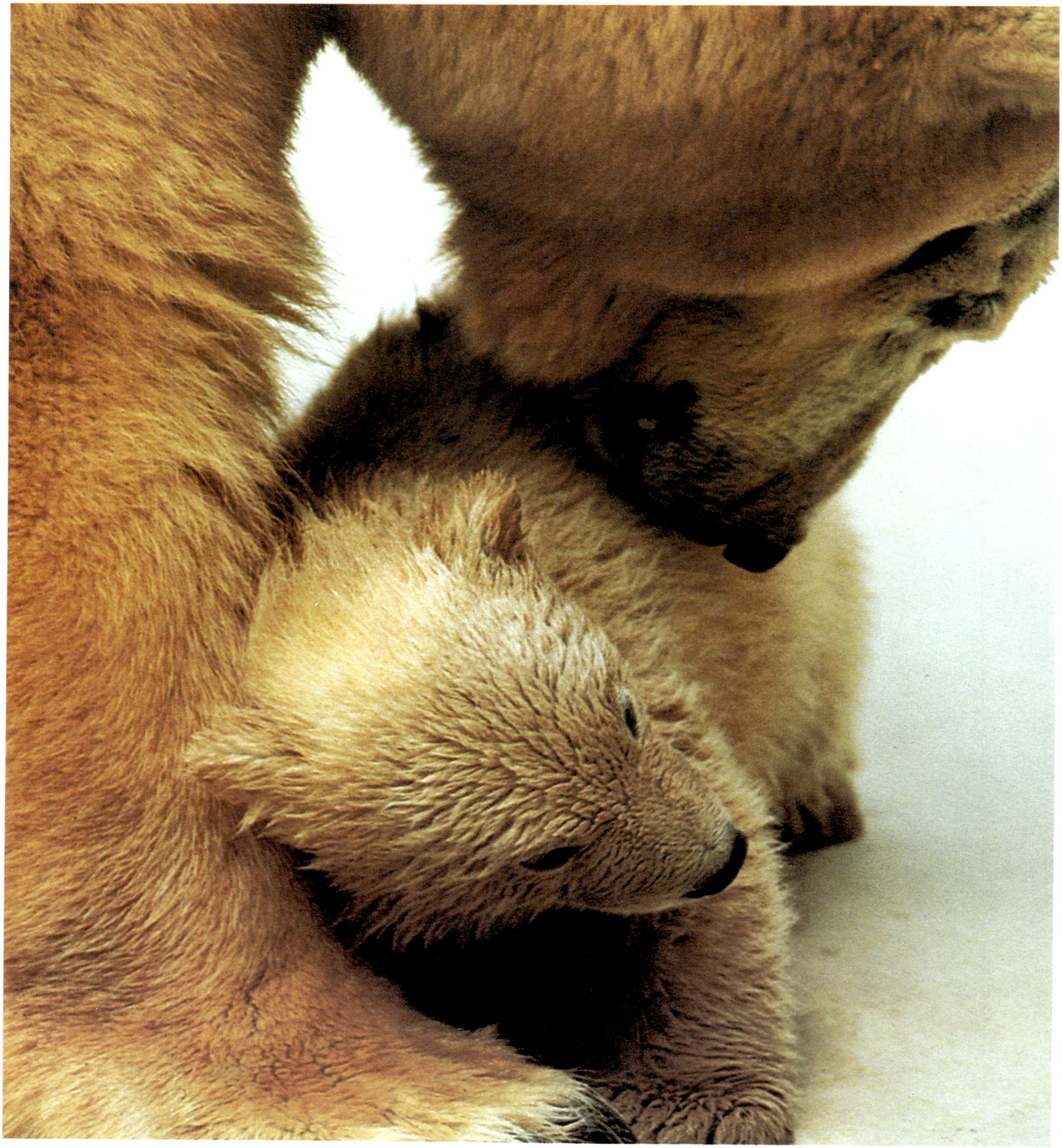

Twin cubs are born in a few weeks. They are the size of a human hand and weigh one pound. They are blind and deaf, have a little hair, and cannot walk. Their mother cleans them with her blue-purple tongue. This prods them to nurse six times a day. Her milk has a rich, nutty flavor.

The cubs stumble around and whimper at first. The sow picks them up gently by the neck. She cuddles them in her paws and cradles them on her back feet. They burrow into her plush fur. She breathes on them to keep them warm.

She repacks the snow often as the cubs grow and gain weight. The family sleeps much of the time. Cubs hear by the 28th day. They see on the 33rd day. They walk after the 46th day.

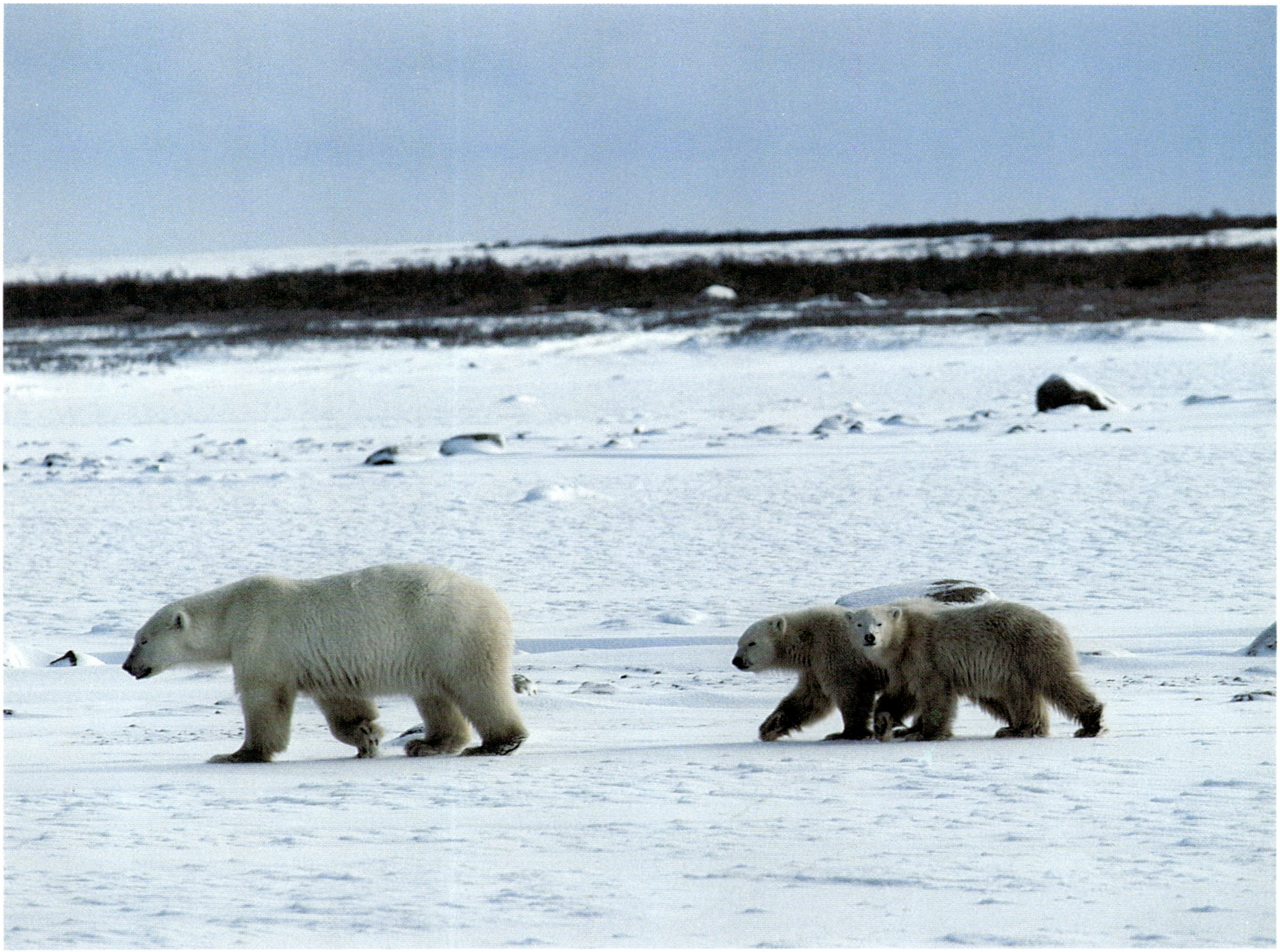

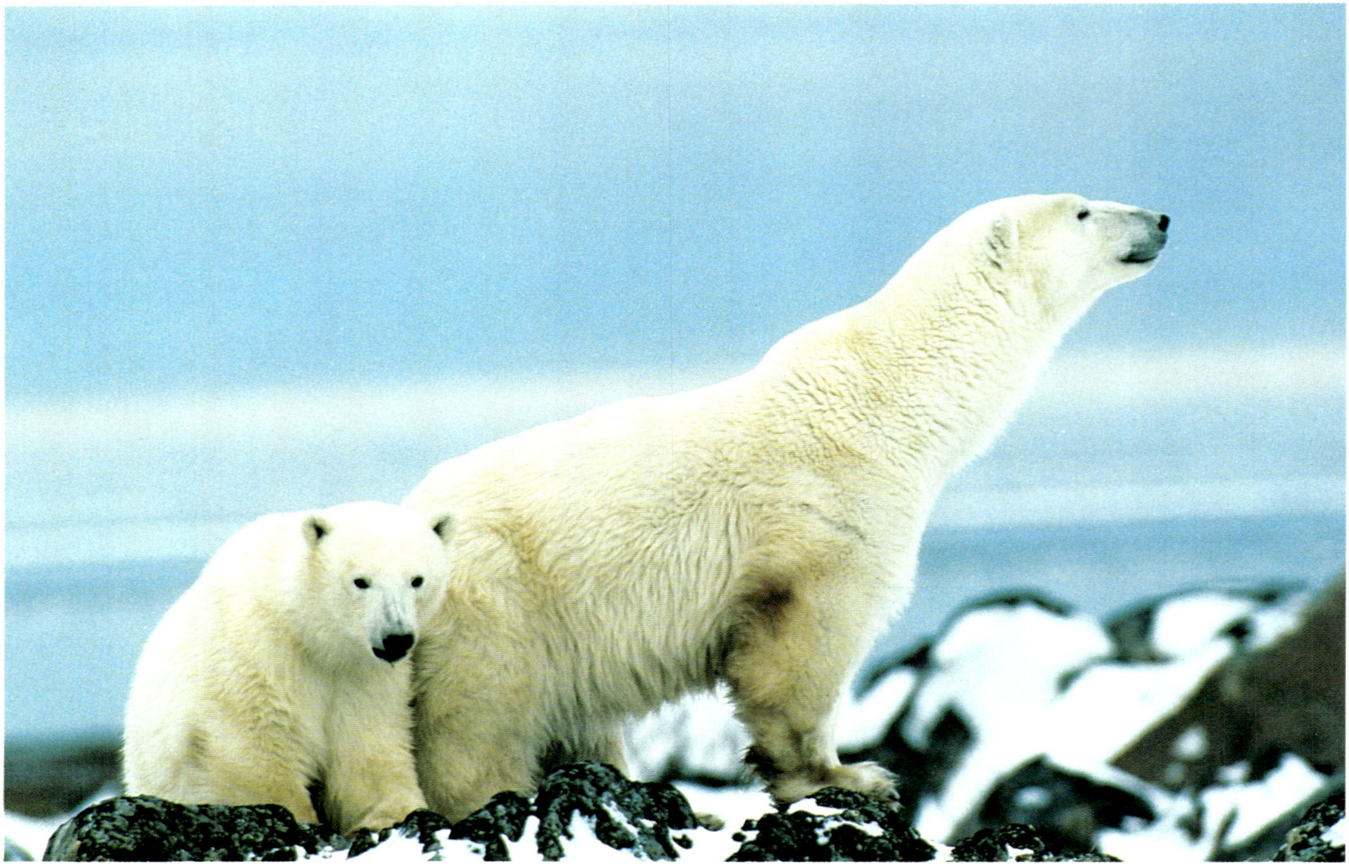

The den is too crowded for all of them after three months. The cubs feel bold and bashful as they greet the world. They explore and play tricks on each other. They tumble, slide, and roll in the snow. Every slope is seen as a giant mountain to climb.

The cubs follow at their mother's heels. She teaches them to survive. Polar bears naturally swim dog-paddle style. She holds them under water so they will get used to it. They whine if she dives out of view. She pulls them back in if they climb out onto the ice. She teaches the cubs to track and hunt.

Mother and cubs "talk" all the time. She roars, growls, and snorts. They bleat, cry, and make little roars. The family stays together for two to three years. Mother pushes the cubs out when she thinks they are ready. They go off to live on their own in their icy world.

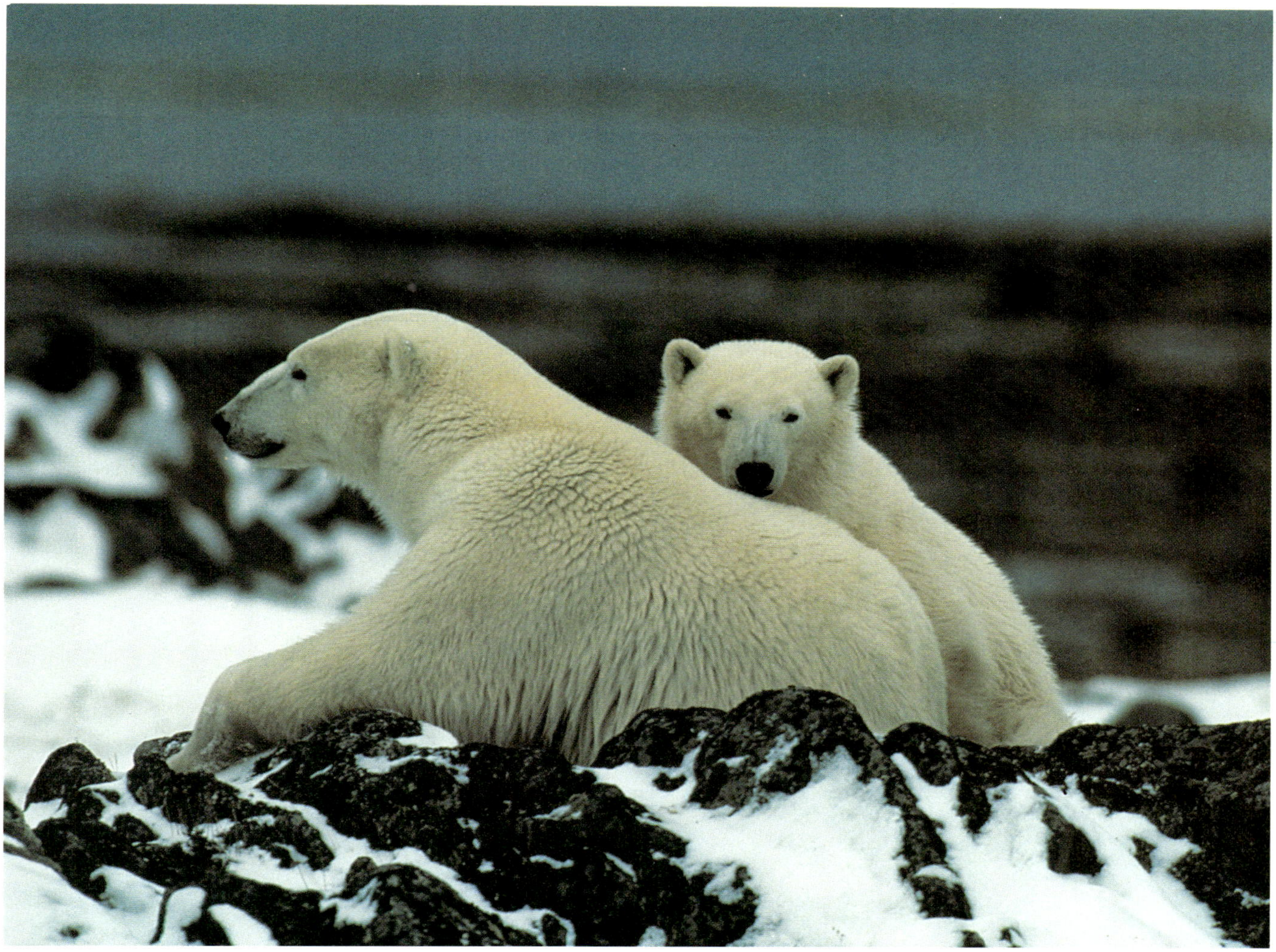

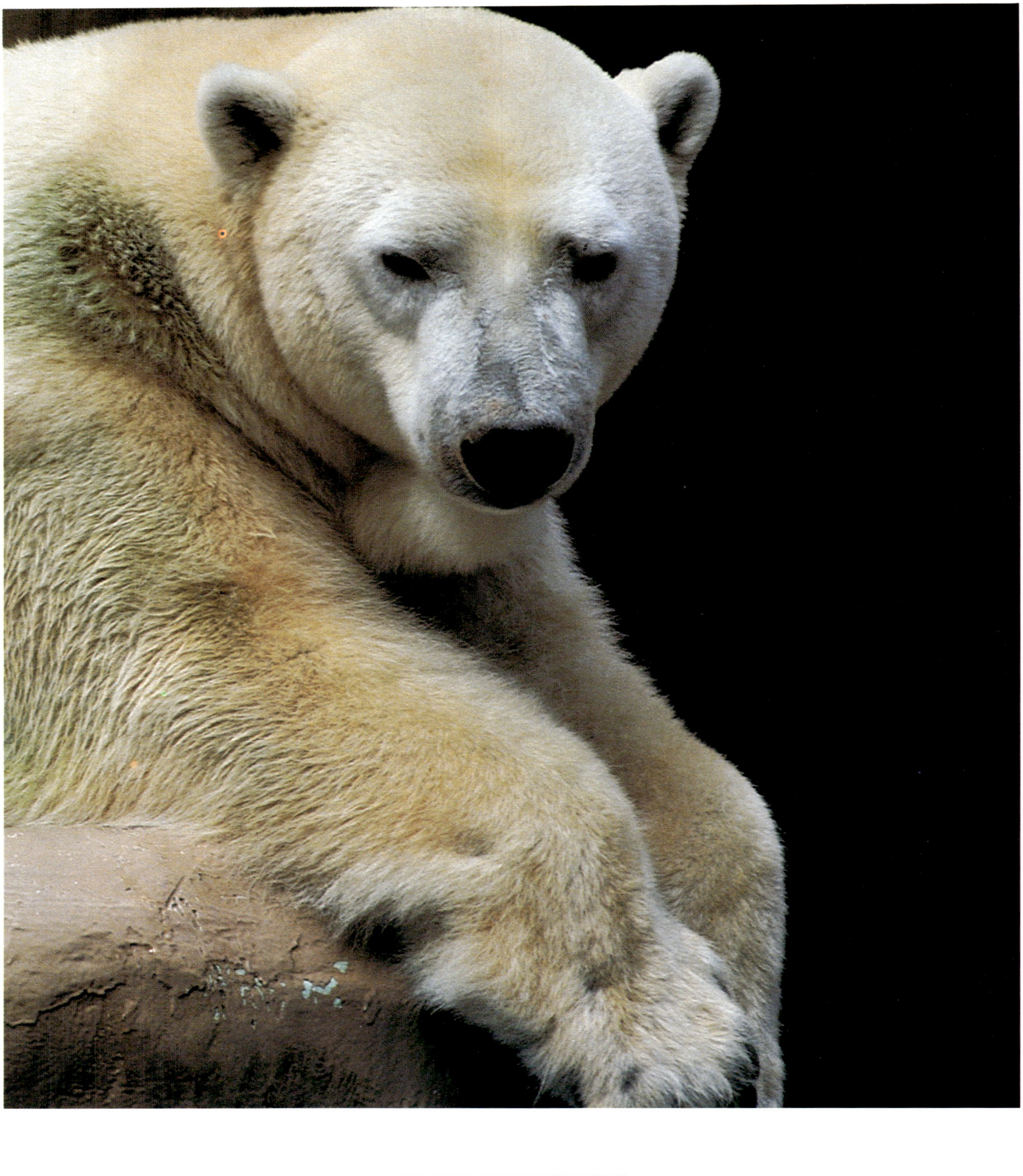

Polar bears do not fear man, who is their one enemy. These animals cannot protect their environment. People must do this for them. All things in nature are connected and have to work together.

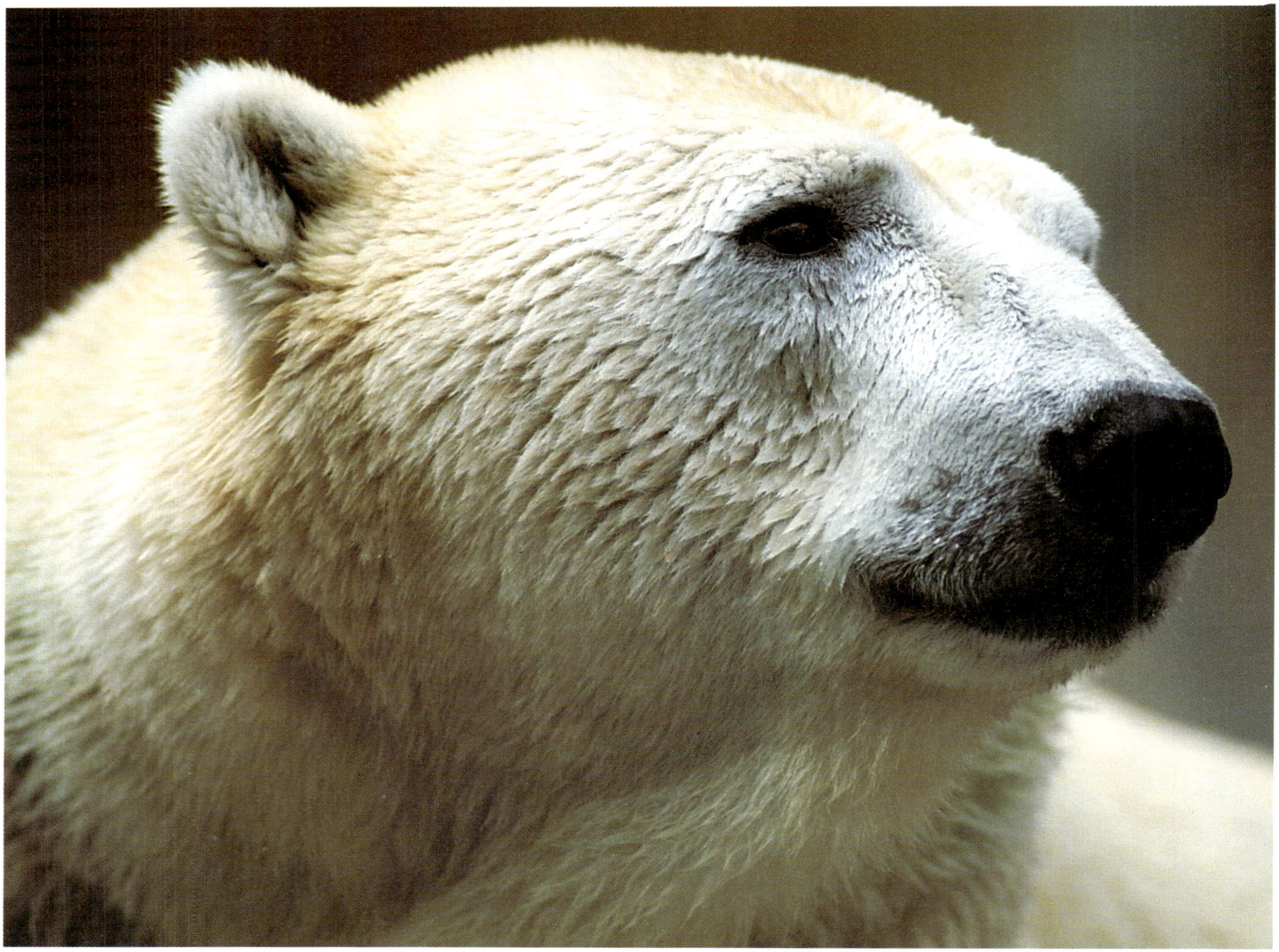

# GLOSSARY / INDEX

**Camouflage**: a form of disguise that blends with the background and makes it hard to be seen (page 6)

**Hibernation**: spending the winter sleeping in an enclosed area (page 18)

**Ice floes**: big chunks that have broken off the ice pack (page 10)

**Migration**: moving from place to place every year at the same time (page 13)

**Outer guard hairs**: long, thick, rough hairs on the top layer of the fur (page 6)

**Pigeon-toed**: feet turn inward toward each other as animal walks (page 13)

**Prey**: animals hunted and killed by another animal for food (page 6)

**Traction**: having a firm grip on a surface (page 9)

**Vessels**: hollow tubes that carry blood through the body (page 6)

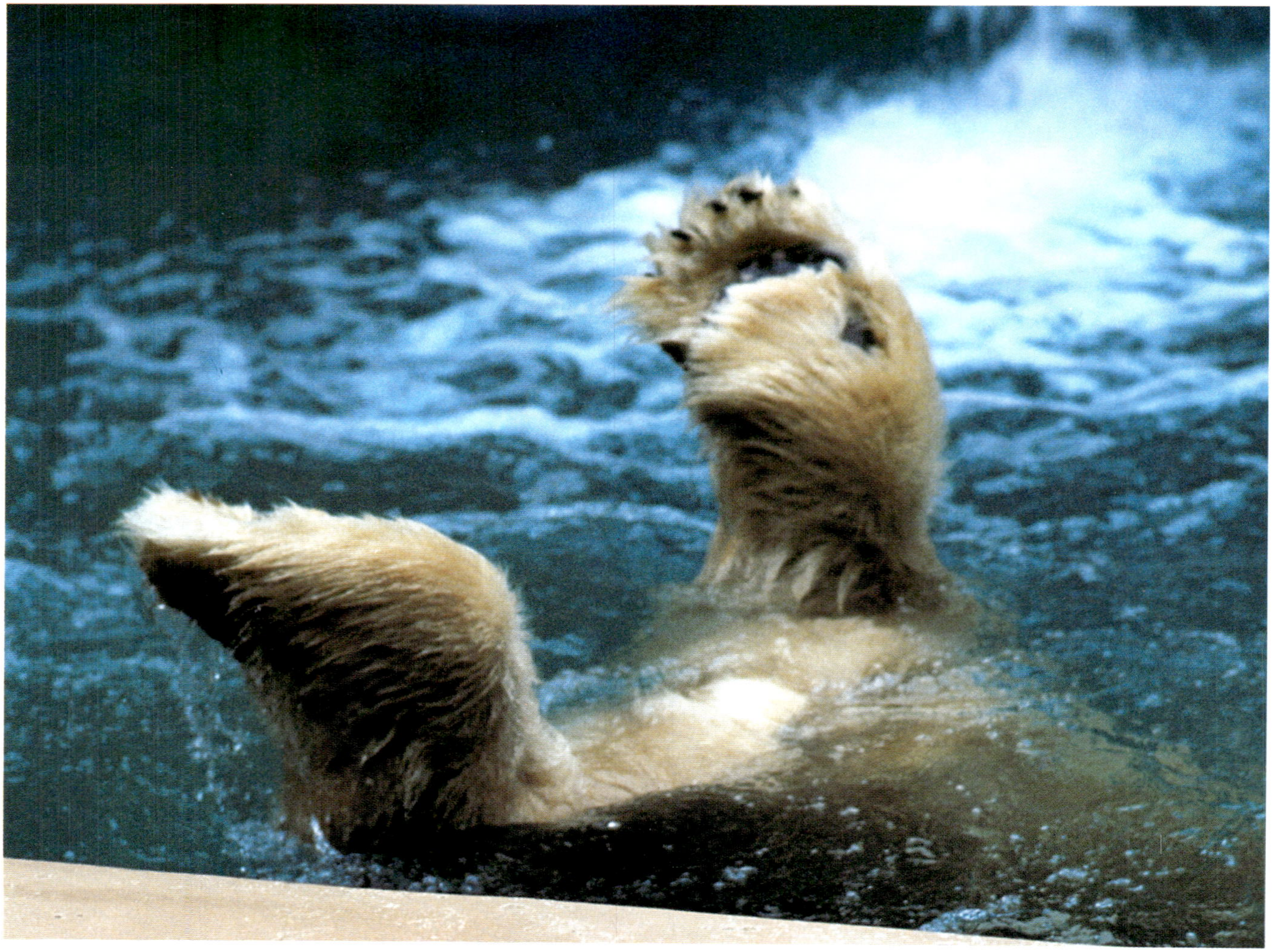